THE
UNBRANDED
STUDENT
WORKBOOK
Reclaiming Your College Search

Dr. Lee Brown
Benjamin P. Roberts

This workbook contains the complete collection of exercises from The Unbranded Student online course. You can find The Unbranded Student book and online course at our website: www.unbrandedstudent.com.

Printed in the United States of America

First Printing, 2019
Unbranded Student
North Richland Hills, Texas 76182
www.unbrandedstudent.com

TABLE OF CONTENTS

INTRODUCTION
(Don't skip this part.)

Welcome to the New Story

If your life were a story, how do you tell the part about going to college?[1] Are you going to the same school the last three generations of your family attended? Have you set your sights on the prestige of an Ivy League school? Are you and your best friend rooming together at a school she picked? Are you a football fan going to your team's school because of the memories you made with your dad on Saturdays watching games?

Our culture tells a story about college too. It goes something like this: If you want to get a good job, you must earn a degree. And if you want your résumé to stand out, you need to go to a prestigious university. But to get into that university, you must make yourself as attractive as possible. You need to have activities and awards and accomplishments to play up in your admissions essays. And, as you have been told non-stop, your college years are some of the best of your life! You belong at a school where you can have the best time, be part of the best programs, and access the best opportunities.

Sound familiar? It's like you're expected to be a brand rather than a person. You have to contort yourself to be just the right kind of person you believe this school wants you to be, instead of the person you are—the unique and wonderful person whose hopes and dreams go far beyond the years you will spend in college.

It's a good story, and parts of it ring true. But most of this story is outdated, shortsighted, and filled with downright lies. And that matters to you because if you base your decisions about college on a faulty or incomplete story, it's bound to affect your own life story too. Most of us aren't in the habit of talking about life as if we're living in a story, but isn't that how we think about the events of our past? The decisions you make about college right now will determine the course of your life. In a sense, they'll write your life story. And don't you want it to be a story of a fulfilling, happy, and successful life? You know by now there are no surefire guarantees of happiness and success, but your choices can set you up for a better chance at getting the life you want.

That's what this workbook is about: We want to tell you a new story. And like any good story, we'll tell you the Five W's: *Who, What, When, Where, Why.* We think you'll like this story. In the old version, the universities have the power—they're the ones who hold the keys and the degrees, and you must make yourself attractive to get their attention.

But in this new story, you're the one with the power.

---

[1] We're assuming your plan is to go to college. It doesn't have to be. There are great options for your future that might not include a university degree. This workbook isn't going to be everything to everyone.

Students are facing huge challenges as they launch their college search. The news is proclaiming skyrocketing student debt, unused college degrees, and rising dropout rate—just to name a few. To manage these challenges, you need to rethink your approach to the entire college-search process.

The truth is, where universities used to pick and choose students, they're now working harder than ever to keep up enrollment. The National Student Clearinghouse reports that student enrollment has dropped for five straight years, and not by a little. "There were just over 18 million students enrolled in higher education nationally in the semester just ended [Spring 2017]—2.4 million fewer than there were in the fall of 2011, the most recent peak."[2]

This means that students—yes, you!—have more power than ever to choose their own path into higher education. We're not talking about waltzing into top-tier universities. We are talking about a new view of what college is and how to get there: Not going to the college your friends are going to. Not going to the college your great-grandfather went to. Not going to the college that will look best on your résumé. And definitely not twisting the facts about yourself and your accomplishments to make a certain university take notice of you. None of these factors are bad in and of themselves, but they're a way of thinking about college as *the end*. We hope to convince you that college can be more—it should be a means to an end rather than an end in itself. What good is a degree if it doesn't align with your unique identity, if it doesn't launch you into a future you're passionate about?

In this workbook, we challenge you to examine your passions, aptitudes, values, and dreams to determine what kinds of schools are the best fit for *you*. When you put all these pieces together, you can take a highly intentional, authentic, and tailored approach to choosing a list of schools that will provide a more fulfilling and successful outcome. With these tools, you can design an ideal path for the kind of life and career you hope to have beyond your college years.

Are you having a hard time buying into this? We created this approach because of what we've seen firsthand through our work in higher education. We've watched these changes happening before our eyes. I (Ben) have sat through countless meetings with college presidents and admissions staff lamenting the drop in enrollment. I (Lee) have watched handfuls of my own students graduate every semester without a plan for how to use their business degree beyond school. College was the goal, and they accomplished it. Now what? They would have been better served if they'd known how to use college as the *tool* to achieve the life they wanted.

We hope you'll hear us out. You have a significant part to play in this new narrative unfolding in higher education. There are a ton of factors you have to think about: the price, the distance from home, the majors offered, the size of the school, the extracurricular activities available … you could make a list so long it could even include the quality of the cafeteria food.

But we believe you don't need to start with a list of schools and compare them on an arbitrary list of attributes. In fact, the college search shouldn't start with a school and work backward—it should start with you, the student. That's what this workbook is all about: allowing students to understand themselves just a little bit better so they have a firm foundation for why they are selecting the college they want to attend.

Are you ready to dive in?

---

[2] Jon Marcus, "Universities and colleges struggle to stem big drops in enrollment," The Hechinger Report, June 29, 2017, http://hechingerreport.org/universities-colleges-struggle-stem-big-drops-enrollment/.

In this workbook, you'll complete five weeks of activities to help you land on the top schools for you. Here's an overview of what you'll discover in the coming weekly modules:

1. Week 1: Who Are You?
2. Week 2: Why?
3. Week 3: Major Discovery
4. Week 4: What Type of College is Right for Me?
5. Week 5: Comparing College Choices

At the end of this work, you will be able to sit down with the people who love you most and explain how the schools you have selected play into the bigger story you want to write for your life.

Let's talk about logistics for a second. This workbook is a combination of the book we wrote for students, *The Unbranded Student: Reclaiming Your College Search*, and activities we offer in our online course. If you would like to register for the online course, you can find it at our website: www.unbrandedstudent.com. Enrolling in the online course will give you access to videos and additional materials that correspond to the coursework in this workbook.

Other books worth buying that will assist in this work are Viktor Frankl's *Man's Search for Meaning* and Gallup's *CliftonStrengths for Students*.

Thanks for taking this journey with us! We're eager to begin.

Regards,

Lee & Ben

Meet the Authors

Who are we to be making such claims? We're Ben and Lee, two guys working in higher education who want to help you make the most of your college experience.

Ben Roberts

I graduated from New York University in 2006 with a Bachelor of Arts and have spent my career working for companies focused on higher education and helping students find their right path. In the last ten years, I have been on over 500 college campuses speaking to presidents and provosts about the best way to recruit students and then ensure those students graduate. Well, that's not the whole story—one sentence in and I'm already keeping something back. Really, my first job out of college was selling Hondas at a small dealership in Texas—more on this story later. I'm passionate about championing the success of international and first-generation students searching for college. Oh, and I got an MBA from Baylor. Most important are my wife, Sara, and my two kids, Moses and Esther.

Lee Brown

After high school, I attended community college for a year before transferring to a large regional university to get my business degree in 2006. Like any pragmatic newly married husband, I took a secure job with the large financial institution I had interned with during school. As it turned out, I learned during the 2008 recession that those large banks were not as stable and predictable as I thought. While working for the bank, I went to school to get my MBA at night and eventually left the industry to pursue a PhD and a job in academia.[3] I now teach at Texas Woman's University, a large regional university within driving distance to most of my family, and I spend my free time with my wife and kids. My educational history is pretty unusual for academia, which is typically obsessed with the diversity and prestige of a candidate's education, but I had a plan for my college education, and it's worked out well for me so far.

---

[3] Thanks to my wonderful wife, who supported me through graduate school while also being an amazing mom to our young kids.

WEEK ONE
Who Are You?

Welcome to Week One of the *Unbranded Student Workbook*, where we ask you a question that seems very simple: Who are you?

To answer this question with more than just your name, you will complete some exercises that help you articulate your strengths, personality, and passions.

We do this to guide your college and career decisions. By the end of this week, you should have a better understanding of how you are wired. When you know who you are, you're better positioned to find careers that are right for YOU!

The Reading: Chapters 1–3 in *The Unbranded Student:*
                        My Story / Find out When / Find out Who

This Week's Work:

- Exercise 1: Understanding Your Personality
  - Take the Meyers–Briggs
  - Take the Enneagram
    - Find both of these at www.unbrandedstudent.com/resources
- Exercise 2: Identifying Your Strengths
- Exercise 3: Extended Strengths Assessment
- Exercise 4: Articulating Your Passions
- Exercise 5: Personality and Career
- Take the Building Block Assessment at www.unbrandedstudent.com/student-quiz

All the work you do this week will allow you to fill out the Unbranded Student Personality Profile. (You can find the personality matrix at the back of this exercise booklet or at www.unbrandedstudent.com/resources).

Next week we'll get into personal mission and success based on how you are unique.

EXERCISE 1
Understanding Your Personality

How are you wired?

Have you ever thought about all the ways your personality impacts your life? It's more than just how you interact with people. Personality affects how you make decisions, the kinds of hobbies you pursue, and what type of work you enjoy. For example, you might have excellent analytical skills, but if you hate spending time alone working on challenging problems until you find an answer, then a job as an actuary or computer scientist probably isn't for you. Because of this, you must consider not only your strengths, but also your personality and passions.

In this section, you'll take the Big Five Personality Test.[4] This personality test is the most popular among researching psychologists. Most of what we know about personality's influence in our lives we learned using this scale. The scale measures five core personality variables in what is called the OCEAN framework:

O – Openness to new experiences
C – Conscientiousness
E – Extroversion
A – Agreeableness
N – Neuroticism (or natural reactions)

Take the test using the link below and fill in your score in the table.
https://www.123test.com/personality-test/

The Big Five Factors	Score
Openness to experience	
Conscientiousness (Work Ethic)	
Extroversion	
Agreeableness	
Natural reactions	

---

[4] There are many different personality tests out there. The one listed above is the most popular test for academics. The most popular test in the career force is the Myers–Briggs. Many people identify with the results, going as far as posting them on their social media profiles. These tests can be very helpful, and if you would like to pay for one or take a free online version, you can, but don't spend the money thinking that the results are the valuable piece. The most valuable part is *the work you do* to reflect on who you are.

Analyze the findings

When you're finished, reflect on the results. Now that you know more about your strengths and your personality, think of ways you have successfully combined the two in a life achievement. If you can't think of an example, imagine a way you might do so in the future. Write it out below. If this is hard to articulate, that's fine, it's supposed to be a little difficult—just think it through.

EXERCISE 2
Identifying Your Strengths

What are your strengths?

In this exercise, we are going to identify your strengths. You'll do this by triangulating the different *domains of engagement*. A domain is something like school, home, work, sports teams, etc.

First, identify your three greatest strengths. Next, ask other people in your life what they perceive to be your strengths—without giving away your own answers. When you hear people in different domains consistently acknowledging similar strengths that confirm you are strong in certain areas, that's not a fluke or context-specific; this is a sign of your true strengths.

For this worksheet, I want you to seek feedback from friends, family, employers, teachers, coaches, and anyone else who interacts with you on a regular basis. It is more helpful if you have some responsibility in the relationship. This can be the traditional responsibility you have to your boss or teacher to complete assigned tasks, or it can be the social responsibility you hold toward friends and family. The point is, you want people with some real investment in your life to guide you.

Log this information in the table below. Find at least four contributors, and record what they say are your three greatest strengths:

Contributor	Strength One	Strength Two	Strength Three

If you want extra credit, get three contributors to fill out the extended assessment on the next page. That will give your contributors a little time to think about their answers and provide more feedback.

Analyze the findings

When you finish collecting the responses, summarize the common themes below. You now have a good idea of what your strengths are and how you are using them in your life. If this confirms what you already know, you are well on your way. If you have strengths in areas where those who know you best aren't seeing them lived out, this is a sign that you should practice using that strength more. We are each wired in different ways and have natural bents, but strengths are built on those bents over time. If you believe you're gifted in an area that you have not been using, find opportunities to build on those strengths—especially if it's something you enjoy.[5]

Common Themes Found in Strength Surveys:

---

[5] If you'd like to take a deep dive into discovering your strengths, the book *CliftonStrengths for Students* is a great resource. When you purchase a new copy of the book, they include a strengths assessment. Many students find this helpful, but remember, identifying strengths is helpful only when you apply what you learn. When you finish this week's module, you will see how strengths are one piece of the puzzle for designing a college experience that supports a career and life you are passionate about.

EXERCISE 3
Extended Strengths Assessment

The three greatest strengths I see in _____ are:

1.	
2.	
3.	

Why these strengths?

Strength 1: _____

_____

_____

Strength 2: _____

_____

_____

Strength 3: _____

_____

_____

EXERCISE 4
Articulating Your Passions

What are you passionate about?[6]

Now that you know more about your strengths and your personality, let's examine what you are uniquely passionate about. This takes a little time and consideration. Generally, in high school, students are willing to join clubs, sports, and other activities in order to stay with friends. This might make you happy through your school years, but it won't help you moving forward. To truly understand what you are passionate about, answer the questions below.

Examine common themes and be mindful of what interests you most. When you're finished, ask a family member if they agree with your results. You know what you are passionate about, but sometimes we skew our passions based on what we see in people we want to emulate. This doesn't make for a happy life.

As a child, I enjoyed doing the following:
I currently enjoy doing the following:
These are things I've always wanted to try:
These are the things I care deeply about:

---

[6] You need to read Viktor Frankl's book *Man's Search for Meaning.*

What are the common themes found in these lists? Why do you find these themes in your life? What do you think these answers say about you?

When you think about getting a job after college, what are possible ways to connect your passions with your natural skills and personality factors?

Now, thinking about your strengths, personality, and passions, let's take a stab at articulating a life mission. You just thought about a job you might enjoy after college, but what is at the core of that job? I work with universities, but when I boil it down to what I really do, it's "to help people find opportunities." For Lee, it's "helping people make wise decisions through researched-based teaching." What is it for you?

EXERCISE 5
Personality and Career

What career would make for an interesting life? Time to combine what you've learned so far!

Now that you have a good idea of your strengths, personality, and passions, you need to find a job that will be a good fit for you. You are unique, so there is no fancy exercise I can provide to lead you there. I need you to think about your situation and develop a list of 3 potential vocations that would be a good fit for your personalities and strengths and could align with your passions in some way. This does not have to be an entry-level position. Try to determine your dream job, and we can always reverse engineer a path to achieving that goal.

Potential Jobs: 1.

_____

2.

_____

3.

_____

Now, I want you to defend your answers below. This will ensure that your logic is sound. Ask yourself: *Why might each job I selected prove to be a good fit for me?*

Job 1:

_____

_____

Job 2:

_____

_____

Job 3:

_____

_____

Finally, on the next page, use what you've learned to fill out your customized Student Personality Profile!

THE UNBRANDED BRIEF
Student Personality Profile

MYERS-BRIGGS		ENNEAGRAM	BUILDING BLOCK
E	Extraversion		
N	Intuition	9	Creative/Polymath
F	Feeling		
J	Judging		

STRENGTHS	BIG FIVE	
Futuristic	OPENNESS	83
Achiever	CONSCIENTIOUSNESS	90
Learner	EXTROVERSION	85
Command	AGREEABLENESS	57
Intellection	NEUROTICISM	28

DREAM JOB

Working with students to pick a college

MAJOR

International Relations

TOP 4 COLLEGES

Yale	UT Austin
Georgetown	NYU

LIFE MISSION

I will use my life to find ways I can help identify opportunities for others.

THE UNBRANDED BRIEF
Student Personality Profile

MYERS-BRIGGS		ENNEAGRAM	BUILDING BLOCK

STRENGTHS

BIG FIVE	
OPENNESS	
CONSCIENTIOUSNESS	
EXTROVERSION	
AGREEABLENESS	
NEUROTICISM	

DREAM JOB
MAJOR
TOP 4 COLLEGES

LIFE MISSION

WEEK TWO
Why?

Welcome to Week Two of the *Unbranded Student Workbook*, where we ask you a question that seems odd: Why?

In the first week of this course, we explored your unique strengths, personality, and passions. This week we ask you to examine your why, which will help you articulate your lifelong mission. Once you have a stronger idea of your mission, you can identify a career type that you will find meaningful.

This is a hard week, but don't worry. Lots of adults have trouble with the activities we will be doing together—not you, though. This can feel intimidating because it requires you to think big and to be willing to evolve over time. But we got your back; we're in this together.

The Reading: Chapter 4 in *The Unbranded Student:* Find Out Why
                        Extra credit if you pick up Frankl's *Man's Search for Meaning.*

This Week's Work:

- Exercise 1: Defining Your Mission
- Exercise 2: Defining Personal Success
- Exercise 3: Goals of Your Heroes
- Exercise 4: Focus & Distractions
- Exercise 5: Writing Your Mission Statement

Next week we will take a deep dive into the variety of college majors out there and the opportunities and pitfalls found in each. You'll be able to pick the one best for you based on the work you've done in weeks one and two.

EXERCISE 1
Defining Your Mission

Developing your mission statement

In this exercise, you'll develop a life mission statement. Organizations use mission statements to clarify what is important to them and what priorities they will pursue. The mission statement isn't just a tool reserved for large organizations; people can benefit from examining their goals and developing a high-level plan for their life.

As you work through this exercise, be sure to create a product that you can use. The mission statement you construct will only be helpful if you can actually use it to guide your decisions. In our work together, we'll use your mission statement to drive your career, major, and college choices in future course lessons.

To get started, summarize the information you gathered during last week's lessons in the table below.

Strengths Summary:

_____

_____

Personality Summary:

_____

_____

Passions Summary:

_____

_____

EXERCISE 2
Defining Personal Success

Living your mission requires you to identify and articulate your gifts and leverage those gifts to reach **your** definition of success. Many people fight their entire lives to find success. When they finally reach this lofty point, they find what they achieved was success as defined by someone else. Nothing is as disparaging as living someone else's dream. In the preface to the 1992 edition of *Man's Search for Meaning*, Viktor Frankl has this to say about success:

> Don't aim at success—the more you aim at it and make it a target, the more you are going to miss it. For Success, like happiness, cannot be pursued; it must ensue, and it only does so as the unintended side-effect of one's dedication to a cause greater than oneself or as the by-product of one's surrender to a person other than oneself. Happiness must happen, and the same holds for success: you have to let it happen by not caring about it. I want you to listen to what your conscience commands you to do and go on to carry it out to the best of your knowledge. Then you will live to see that in the long run—in the long run, I say!—success will follow you precisely because you had *forgotten* to think of it. (Frankl, XIV–XV)

The reality is, when you are mission-driven, when you are committed to your cause, success is the happy by-product. Answer the questions below to help you determine what success means for you.

Define Success:

_____

_____

_____

_____

List 4 components of your view of success:

_____

_____

_____

_____

What does success look like to you at various ages?

Age 25? _____

_____

_____

Age 35? _____

_____

_____

Age 55? _____

_____

_____

EXERCISE 3
Goals of Your Heroes

It's important to find people who have accomplished what you want to achieve. This helps put in perspective the time it will take for you to accomplish something and make you aware of the hours of practice and effort ahead of you.

Take some time to think of three people who have attained the success you want for your life. Think deeply about each person and what you know about their history. Write down three goals they would have used to guide their path to success.

1. Person: _____

Goal: _____

Goal: _____

Goal: _____

2. Person: _____

Goal: _____

Goal: _____

Goal: _____

3. Person: _____

Goal: _____

Goal: _____

Goal: _____

EXERCISE 4
Focus & Distractions

Mission statement

Now that you have a clear sense of what success looks like for *you*, it's time to craft your mission statement. Navigating life decisions is easier when you know what you're working toward—that's what a mission statement does for you. Before you decide to take on a responsibility, accept a new opportunity, or join an activity, first determine if it fits within your mission. If it doesn't, then the activity may be a waste of time on your journey. This is why thinking deeply about your mission is so important: if you believe in your mission, you live according to its precepts.

Keep in mind that you will grow. Be sure to create a mission statement that can evolve with your changing priorities and circumstances in life. Don't be discouraged when the things you have to do seem to take you away from your mission. One of the attributes you have as an emerging leader is the wisdom to take advantage of any situation and make it support your path to the successful life you dream of.

Mission focus

List five critical things you must focus on to achieve your definition of success.

1. _____

2. _____

3. _____

4. _____

5. _____

What values do you hold dear? What is more important to you than anything else?

1. _____

2. _____

3. _____

4. _____

5. _____

Distractions

Now, think about the things that will distract your focus and derail you from achieving your definition of success and fulfilling your vision. These are often things that *seem* important. Understand this early in order to stay on the right path. List three distractions and the effect they will have on your life if you continue to focus on them:

1. Distraction _____

Impact: _____

_____

_____

2. Distraction: _____

Impact: _____

_____

_____

3. Distraction: _____

Impact: _____

_____

_____

EXERCISE 5
Writing Your Mission Statement

Considering the strength, personality, and passion factors that make you unique, develop a one- or two-sentence mission statement to help guide your life decisions.[7] This mission should guide your life decisions including your college choice.[8]

---

[7] Ben's mission is to help people find opportunities. Lee's mission is to help people make wise decisions through research-based teaching. What's yours?

[8] If later on you recognize that your life does not seem to be aligned with the mission that you wrote, it is time to reevaluate and take one of two options: (1) You realize that you have changed, so you go back and update your mission. (2) You realize that you are floating through life and not living with the intention that you should. Use your mission statement to realign!

WEEK THREE
Major Discovery

Welcome to Week Three of the *Unbranded Student Workbook*, where we will get down to the What. The What is picking a major that matches your unique self.

In this week, we will think about different career paths, specifically looking for the knowledge, skills, and abilities needed to succeed. Once we have identified your potential careers, we will create a life plan for how you can develop the skills needed for those careers over the next four years. College will be the main tool we use for doing this, but this strategic approach to college planning will also point out what skills you will not be able to gain from a certain degree program. You can supplement gaps that are intrinsic to certain degrees by using your free electives or a minor to fill in areas you will need for your career.

Reading: Chapter 5 in *The Unbranded Student:* Find Out What

This Week's Work:

- Exercise 1: What Will It Take to Achieve the Dream Career?
- Exercise 2: What Did Others Do?
- Exercise 3: Analyze College Majors Based on Career

At the end of this week, you should have a good idea of how the career you want to pursue matches potential majors.

Next week we look at school types and identifying the best type of school for you.

EXERCISE 1
What Will It Take to Achieve the Dream Career?

Describe your dream career:

What knowledge, skills, or abilities do you need to succeed in your chosen career? Visit www.onetonline.org/skills/ to understand the interplay between skills and jobs, and record your answers below.

EXERCISE 2
What Did Others Do?

The only way to know how to get into your dream career is to talk to people who have done it. Use the interview questions below to guide a discussion with someone who is where you want to be. Extra points if you are able to find someone in their 30s and someone in their 60s to understand the journey the career takes.

How did you land this job?

_____

Where did you go to school, and what was your major?

_____

Was that major the best fit for what you are doing now?

_____

What's the best thing about this job? What's the worst thing about this job?

_____

What do you wish you would have known before going to college?

_____

Do you feel like this career makes the best use of your strengths?

_____

What advice would you give me as I consider pursuing this career?

_____

EXERCISE 3
Analyze College Majors Based on Career

What majors seem right for me?

_____

_____

Why these majors?

_____

_____

_____

What knowledge, skills, and abilities identified in Week One will I gain from my college degree?

_____

_____

_____

What gaps do I anticipate needing to fill that my major does not provide?

_____

_____

_____

_____

What is my plan to supplement my education and ensure I have everything I need to succeed?

_____

_____

WEEK FOUR
What Type of College is Right for Me?

Welcome to Week Four of the *Unbranded Student Workbook*. It's getting serious now, because this week we are going to start thinking: Where? In order to decide what school is best for you, you should first understand the different types of schools available.

So far, you have spent time in deep self-reflection, decided on a possible career that might interest you, and examined the college majors that might work for you, making sure they align with the dreams you have for your life. With this information, you are now ready to choose what type of university you will attend.

Do you see the difference in the method you've used to get here? Most approaches to the college decision-making process encourage you to choose the school first and then make everything else fit. That is one reason so many people are obtaining degrees and then slogging through careers that are unfulfilling. You, on the other hand, are now equipped with the information to make a wise decision about which college to attend.

In this week, we will identify different types of colleges and universities and examine the benefits and downsides of each kind. You will use this information to develop a list of the types of institutions you expect to attend.

The Reading: Chapter 6 in *The Unbranded Student:* Find out Where

This Week's Work:

- Exercise 1: Picking the Right Type of College
- Exercise 2: Interviewing Colleges

Take it easy this week—next week is going to be a lot of work.

EXERCISE 1
Picking the Right Type of College

What do I want to get out of my university experience?

_____

_____

_____

What are my expectations of my professors?

_____

_____

_____

What's the ten-year career plan after college?

_____

_____

_____

What are the most important things my college can do to help me succeed?

_____

_____

_____

Which type of college is the best fit for my situation? Why?

_____

_____

_____

Which type of college is the second-best fit for my situation? Why?

_____

_____

_____

Which type of college is the third-best fit for my goals? Why?

_____

_____

_____

Which type of college would be completely wrong for me? Why?

_____

_____

_____

EXERCISE 2
Interviewing Colleges

For this exercise, your task is to call three colleges that fall into the college type category you identified as being the best fit for you. You'll need to ask a different set of questions for each type of college you interview, but you can use the questions below as a starting point. The best place to start calling is the admissions office. You can always find their number on the college's website.

What does orientation look like?

What is the advising model? Do faculty advise students, or is it primarily professional advisors?

What makes you most proud of the college?

What's the best thing about this university? What's the worst thing about this university?

What types of students have you seen succeed here?

What's the best advice you'd give a student considering attending this college?

WEEK FIVE
Comparing College Choices

Welcome to Week Five of the *Unbranded Student Workbook*—the final week. This week we arrive at the point of the college search process most people begin with: the list of colleges you want to consider.

Now, using what you have developed in previous weeks, you have all the appropriate analysis in place to make a wise decision about where you will attend college. Does your college choice make sense for your situation? We will use the exercises in today's lesson to highlight the opportunity cost of your decisions. In this section, you will take the college analysis that you made in Week Four and apply it to your unique situation. Understand that this is an iterative process. You might have found the perfect school for you, but if the math doesn't work, you need to either find scholarship money (renewable for ALL 4 years!) that fixes the math problem or make another choice.

Reading: Chapter 7 in *The Unbranded Student:* Go Forth

This Week's Work:

- Exercise: **The Unbranded College Search Matrix**

On these final pages you will find **The Unbranded College Search Matrix**. This brings together everything you have learned about yourself. We have taken a stab at doing one for you so you can see how it works. We provided five additional blank matrixes for you to fill out with your top five college choices. You can find additional information and matrixes at www.unbrandedstudent.com/resources.

THE UNBRANDED COLLEGE SEARCH MATRIX

What do I want to accomplish with my degree?

While I'm at college I want the opportunity to be involved in intermural sports, take some art classes to explore my interests in painting, and most importantly find a job working with international businesses when I graduate. I've struggled in high school with finding the right support with my dyslexia, so it is critical I find a place that can help me from time to time.

What do I want to major in?

International Business

What are the three most important things about the college I enroll in?

1. *A solid career management office that can help me get an internship with an international business.*
2. *A lively student life community that provides activities.*
3. *A student support office that is open and flexible.*

How am I weighting the points to select the front-runner?

If we created the points or relied on top 20 lists, it wouldn't be a search for you.

I will use a 1–5 point scale, with each item weighted the same to get a total value.

THE UNBRANDED COLLEGE SEARCH MATRIX

College	College of the UNIQUE		Party College USA		Notes
College Metric	Answer	Points	Answer	Points	
Average Annual Cost	$36,000	2	$38,000	3	Find this data at www.collegescorecard.ed.gov (CS)
Average Time to Degree	5 years	3	4.5 Years	5	
Anticipated Total Cost	$180,000	2	$171,500	3	This is just annual cost multiplied by average time to degree
Average Debt at Graduation	$24,250	1	$36,000	5	CS again
Average four-year Graduation Rate	70%	3	73%	3	CS- you can look at four or six year based on how quick you want out
Average Salary after Attending	$58,000	5	$44,000	3	CS – take into account what job you want to think about the average
Does it offer my major?	It's selective, I might get in my major after two years, no promise	2	Yes	5	College Website
Does it accomplish important thing 1	Great Career Services	5	Okay career services, but good alumni network	4	You created these on the other page
Does it accomplish important thing 2	I have some people I know attending	4	Lots of Greek life, not my preference	1	
Does it accomplish important thing 3	Good services for tutoring	3	Good services for tutoring	3	

I'm doing two on page here to show comparison, but for yours it's one matrix for each school you are considering.

EXAMPLE

THE UNBRANDED COLLEGE SEARCH MATRIX

College	College of the UNIQUE		Party College USA		Notes
College Metric	Answer	Points	Answer	Points	
Will I find a community here?	Yes	5	Depends on getting into a frat	1	Probably need to visit for this, or call and interview the school
Will I be able to use my strengths? How?	Yes, good leadership opportunities	5	Yes, has a debate team	3	This is all you
Will I be excited to go to this school?	It's so close to home	1	Yes	5	
I'm most excited by this school because…	Huge national reputation	4	Living in a big city	5	
What are the consequences of missteps?	Lots of people spend an extra year here because they change majors	-4	None I can find	3	What happens if you take the wrong class? Don't enroll in time? Call the school and ask to talk to an advisor about your specific major and what it takes to be successful. Ask – What do most students do wrong? This is negative question, it has negative points.
I'm most worried about this school because…	I'm tired of living in this town	-2	I'm nervous what it means if I don't get into a frat	-5	All you, friend. But this is a negative question, so it needs negative points.
Total Points		38		48	This is sum of all points

EXAMPLE

THE UNBRANDED COLLEGE SEARCH MATRIX

What do I want to accomplish with my degree?

What do I want to major in?

What are the three most important things about the college I enroll in?

    1.

    2.

    3.

How am I weighting the points to select the front-runner?
If we created the points or relied on top 20 lists, it wouldn't be a search for you.

THE UNBRANDED COLLEGE SEARCH MATRIX

College	Answer	Points
College Metric		
Average Annual Cost		
Average Time to Degree		
Average Total Cost		
Average Debt at Graduation		
Average four-year Graduation Rate		
Average Salary after Attending		
Does it offer my major?		
Does it accomplish important thing 1		
Does it accomplish important thing 2		
Does it accomplish important thing 3		

THE UNBRANDED COLLEGE SEARCH MATRIX

College		
College Metric	Answer	Points
Will I find a community here?		
Will I be able to use my strengths? How?		
Will I be excited to go to this school?		
I'm most excited by this school because…		
What are the consequences of missteps?		
I'm most worried about this school because…		
Total Points		

THE UNBRANDED COLLEGE SEARCH MATRIX

College		Points
College Metric	Answer	
Average Annual Cost		
Average Time to Degree		
Average Total Cost		
Average Debt at Graduation		
Average four-year Graduation Rate		
Average Salary after Attending		
Does it offer my major?		
Does it accomplish important thing 1		
Does it accomplish important thing 2		
Does it accomplish important thing 3		

THE UNBRANDED COLLEGE SEARCH MATRIX

College		
College Metric	Answer	Points
Will I find a community here?		
Will I be able to use my strengths? How?		
Will I be excited to go to this school?		
I'm most excited by this school because…		
What are the consequences of missteps?		
I'm most worried about this school because…		
Total Points		

THE UNBRANDED COLLEGE SEARCH MATRIX

College		Points
College Metric	Answer	
Average Annual Cost		
Average Time to Degree		
Average Total Cost		
Average Debt at Graduation		
Average four-year Graduation Rate		
Average Salary after Attending		
Does it offer my major?		
Does it accomplish important thing 1		
Does it accomplish important thing 2		
Does it accomplish important thing 3		

THE UNBRANDED COLLEGE SEARCH MATRIX

College		
College Metric	Answer	Points
Will I find a community here?		
Will I be able to use my strengths? How?		
Will I be excited to go to this school?		
I'm most excited by this school because…		
What are the consequences of missteps?		
I'm most worried about this school because…		
Total Points		

THE UNBRANDED COLLEGE SEARCH MATRIX

College Metric	Answer	Points
Average Annual Cost		
Average Time to Degree		
Average Total Cost		
Average Debt at Graduation		
Average four-year Graduation Rate		
Average Salary after Attending		
Does it offer my major?		
Does it accomplish important thing 1		
Does it accomplish important thing 2		
Does it accomplish important thing 3		

THE UNBRANDED COLLEGE SEARCH MATRIX

College		
College Metric	Answer	Points
Will I find a community here?		
Will I be able to use my strengths? How?		
Will I be excited to go to this school?		
I'm most excited by this school because…		
What are the consequences of missteps?		
I'm most worried about this school because…		
Total Points		

THE UNBRANDED COLLEGE SEARCH MATRIX

College	Answer	Points
College Metric		
Average Annual Cost		
Average Time to Degree		
Average Total Cost		
Average Debt at Graduation		
Average four-year Graduation Rate		
Average Salary after Attending		
Does it offer my major?		
Does it accomplish important thing 1		
Does it accomplish important thing 2		
Does it accomplish important thing 3		

THE UNBRANDED COLLEGE SEARCH MATRIX

College		
College Metric	Answer	Points
Will I find a community here?		
Will I be able to use my strengths? How?		
Will I be excited to go to this school?		
I'm most excited by this school because...		
What are the consequences of missteps?		
I'm most worried about this school because...		
Total Points		

Made in the USA
Coppell, TX
07 January 2022

71071498R00031